# Simpson and his Donkey

Mark Greenwood    Frané Lessac

WALKER BOOKS
AND SUBSIDIARIES
LONDON • BOSTON • SYDNEY • AUCKLAND

Jack and Billy grew up in the back lanes of Tyne Dock, where a river carried great ships out to sea.

During summer holidays they led donkeys along the seaside trail for a penny a ride. From morning 'til twilight they paced the sands of South Shields, whistling Geordie tunes for passengers balanced on the donkeys' backs.

In winter Jack carted milk to support his family. With a ring of his bell he worked the cobbled streets, taking payment with his frozen fingers. In the harbour, freighters and tugs sounded off with toots and whistles. Jack dreamed that one day he would sail away on a great adventure.

‘There’s neh need t’worry,’ he told Billy, ‘aa’ll not forget yee.’

At seventeen Jack signed up as a stoker on a ship bound for Australia.

He beat his way through the bush with a swag and a billy can.

He cut cane and rode the boundary of a cattle station.

He laboured in coalmines, then joined the gold rush.

But Jack never dug a fortune from the ground. Instead he returned to the sea. Down in the bowels of a steamship, Jack fed the furnace.

*Ah wish ah was 'ome*, he thought,
*every bird likes its own nest.*

Jack was enjoying a spell ashore when he heard the news that England and Germany were at war. He was quick to enlist in the army. It was a chance to do his duty for king and country – and a ticket home quicker than planned.

Jack trained as a stretcher-bearer but the troops sailed for Egypt, not England, as he'd hoped. In the shadow of ancient pyramids, soldiers practised for battle. Jack marched through the desert and treated mock wounded at a dressing station pitched among the palms.

When Turkey entered the war, British commanders drew up plans to launch an invasion on the Gallipoli Peninsula.

*You'll find out where ah am when the Australians make a start*, Jack wrote to his mother.

On a moonless April morning, a fleet of destroyers steamed towards the Turkish coast. Steel hulls formed a line facing the landing point. Jack climbed down a rope ladder into a crowded rowboat.

Pale-faced soldiers confessed their faith as the convoy approached the rugged, clay-faced cliffs. Enemy gunfire sparked from the scrub-covered ridges.

Jack's heart pounded. 'Ah wish ah was 'ome in canny old Shields,' he whispered.

At dawn the boats grounded on a pebbled seabed.

Turkish machine guns snickered, whipping up spouts of water. Jack felt the zip of a bullet pass by his head. He tumbled into the icy Aegean Sea and waded to shelter beneath an overhang.

Soldiers stormed the beach under orders to secure higher ground. They fixed bayonets and charged up the razorback ridges. Enemy artillery exploded overhead, showering the cove with fiery shrapnel.

Exposed to bullet and bomb, Jack edged along narrow tracks to evacuate a constant stream of wounded to lifeboats that lined the shore.

The first aid station at Hell Spit was unprepared for the mounting casualties. Stretchers soon became a scarce commodity.

Jack was responding to a cry for help when he came upon a donkey cowering in a gully of pines. A shell burst high above, spitting out a hail of metal. Jack ignored the concussion of artillery and crawled across the shell-torn ground.

'Bless yee little fella,' he whispered into a long fluffy ear, and he christened his frightened friend 'Duffy'.

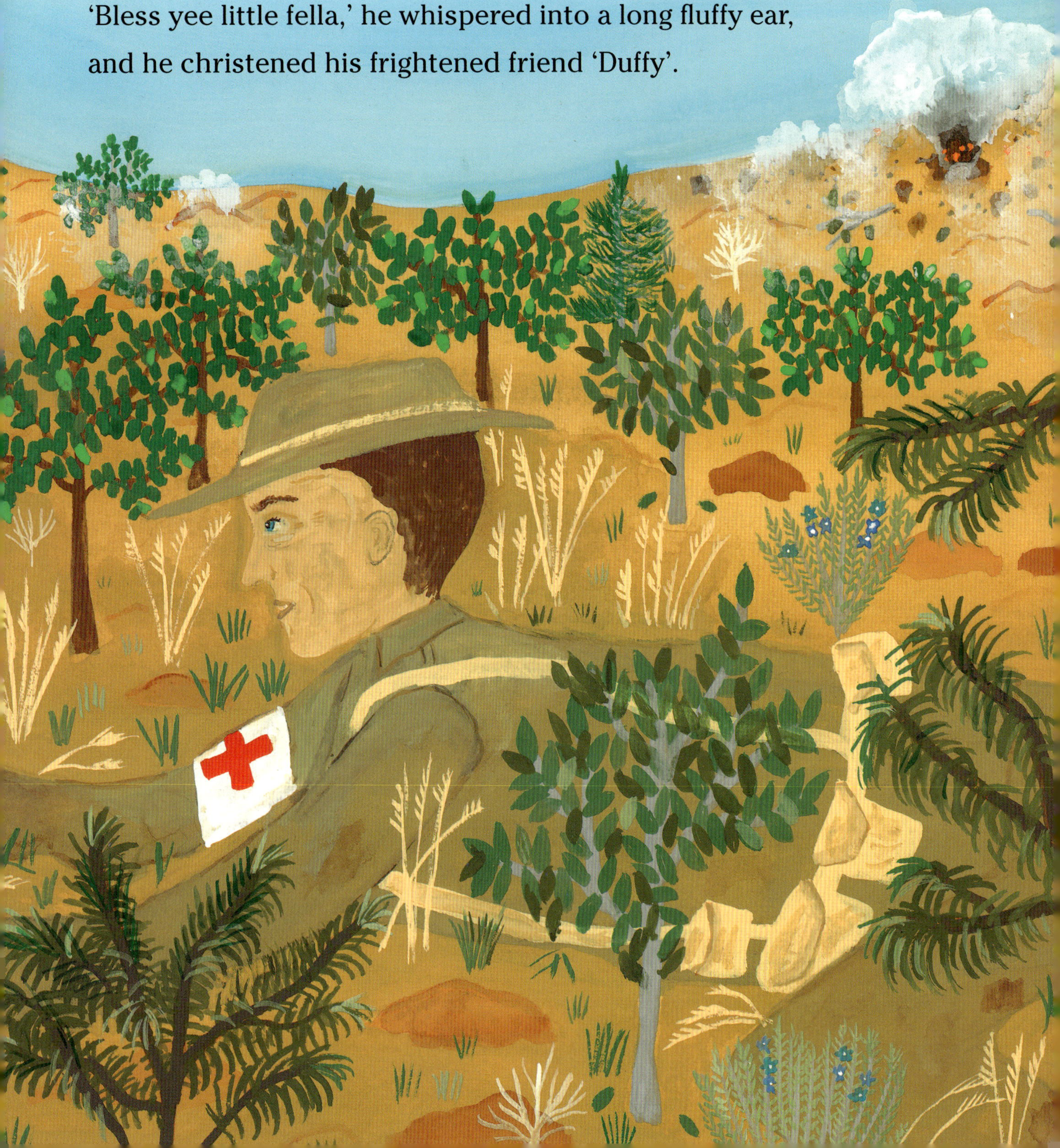

Within reach of a dozen enemy rifles, a soldier raised his bloodied arm. Jack leapt over craters gouged into the battlefield, dodging shot and shell.

'It doesn't do to linger in nasty spots like this,' he said. Jack gently lifted his patient onto the donkey's back.

He guided Duffy with a lead rope fashioned from field dressings and picked his way down the stony ravine.

That was the first of many brave rescues. In sunshine or drizzling rain, Jack Simpson marched up Shrapnel Valley with Duffy by his side. They made twelve to fifteen trips each day, carrying water to thirsty troops, returning with a soldier straddled over the donkey's back.

At night Jack guided Duffy by lantern light down the zigzag track and camped with an Indian artillery unit. The Sikh gunners named him Bahadur – *Bravest of the Brave*.

Simpson and his donkey earned the admiration of all who watched them work. The colonel decorated Duffy's forehead with a Red Cross armband. 'You're worth a hundred men to me,' he said.

On the morning of May 19th, Turkish forces launched a fierce assault. It seemed a miracle that anyone could survive when the air was hazy with lead.

‘Snipers are busy in the gully ahead,’ warned a soldier.
‘It’s hot as hell up there.’

‘Aa’ll be aalreet,’ said Jack with a wave.
‘Have breakfast ready when ah get back.’

With the rising sun behind him, a Turkish soldier took aim and slowly squeezed the trigger. His target was leading a donkey up a steep incline at the junction of Dead Man's Ridge.

The bullet struck Jack in the back and passed through his heart. Soldiers dragged their mate to the side of the track, and word passed down the line.

In
Loving
Memory
JACK SIMPSON AMC

Battle-weary men were misty-eyed when Duffy trudged down the valley alone. Indian gunners risked their lives to gather a wreath of poppies to decorate a wooden cross. A hush descended over the battlefield. In the maze of terraced dugouts, candles flickered like evening stars the night Jack Simpson was buried at Hell Spit.

Jack rescued over three hundred men during twenty-four days. Among them was an English soldier who grew up in the back lanes of Tyne Dock.

'There's neh need t'worry,' Jack had called out over the stutter of gunfire. 'Aa'll not forget yee.'

Jack supported the wounded man to prevent him slipping from the donkey. With Duffy trotting by his side, Jack smiled and whistled a Geordie tune, and led Billy through the valley of death.

*Lest We Forget.*

## JOHN SIMPSON KIRKPATRICK
### (KNOWN AS JACK)

| | | | |
|---|---|---|---|
| **NICKNAMES:** | | | |
| Jacky, Simmo, Murphy, Scotty, Simmie | | | |
| **DATE AND PLACE OF BIRTH:** | | | |
| July 6th, 1892, South Shields, County Durham, England | | | |
| **MILITARY UNIT:** | | | |
| 3rd Field Ambulance, Australian Army Medical Corps | | | |
| **NUMBER:** | 202 | **RANK:** | Private |
| **DATE AND PLACE OF DEATH:** | | | |
| May 19th, 1915, Shrapnel Valley, Gallipoli, Turkey | | | |
| **CEMETERY:** | | | |
| Gallipoli 30, Beach Cemetery, Anzac Cove | | | |

Jack spoke with a Geordie accent which identified him as someone born within sight of the River Tyne (north-east England).

## THE DONKEYS

Jack sometimes used other donkeys to give Duffy a rest. He gave them a variety of names: Murphy, Abdul and Queen Elizabeth. But his favourite was Duffy. At a ceremony at the Australian War Memorial on May 19th, 1997, the Purple Cross was awarded posthumously to all the donkeys for exceptional work performed while under continual fire at Gallipoli.

## BILLY LOWES

Able seaman William (Billy) Lowes joined the Nelson Battalion, Royal Navy. His division, sent to reinforce the Anzacs, landed on April 29th. Four days later he was wounded.

Lapsing in and out of consciousness, he remembered being taken down to the beach dressing station on a donkey.

'We used to play together as children but I did not recognise Jack at the time,' he said. 'Shot and shell were flying all around when Jack struck across my path and brought me in on his donkey.'

## MASCOTS

The Australian soldiers believed kangaroos and other animals would bring them good luck.

When they travelled abroad to fight in the war, they brought mascots from home to raise their spirits and help them feel less homesick.

## THE TURKS

From April to December 1915, more than one million Allied and Turkish soldiers fought on the battlefields of Gallipoli. One in two was either wounded or killed. The people of Turkey know it as the Battle of Çanakkale.

The Turkish soldiers defended their homeland with much courage and honour and the Australian and New Zealand soldiers regarded their opponents with great respect.

In some places the trenches were so close, the Anzacs could hear the Turks singing songs in the evening. Sometimes the soldiers exchanged food and gifts.

## GENERAL MUSTAFA KEMAL ATATÜRK

The Battle of Çanakkale was where the great Turkish leader, General Mustafa Kemal Atatürk, led his troops to victory over the Allied forces. Atatürk expressed the bond between the soldiers from all nations with these famous words:

'Those heroes who shed their blood and lost their lives, you are now lying in the soil of a friendly country. Therefore rest in peace. There is no difference between the Johnnies and the Mehmets to us where they lie side by side in this country of ours. You, the mothers, who sent their sons from far away countries, wipe away your tears; your sons are now lying in our bosom and are in peace. After having lost their lives on this land they become our sons as well.'

ANZAC COVE, TURKEY 1915

*For the soldiers from all nations who fought and died at Gallipoli*

First published in 2008
by Walker Books Australia Pty Ltd
Locked Bag 22, Newtown
NSW 2042 Australia
www.walkerbooks.com.au

This edition published in 2011.



National Library of Australia Cataloguing-in-Publication entry:

Greenwood, Mark.
Simpson and his donkey / Mark Greenwood; illustrator, Frané Lessac.
ISBN: 978 1 921529 54 2 (pbk.)
For primary school aged children.
Subjects: Kirkpatrick, John Simpson, 1892-1915 – Juvenile literature.
Australia. Army. Field Ambulance, 3rd – Juvenile literature.
World War, 1914-1918 – Campaigns – Turkey – Gallipoli Peninsula – Juvenile literature.
Other Authors/Contributors: Lessac, Frané.

940.426092

Typeset in Cheltenham Book
Printed and bound in China

10 9 8 7 6 5 4 3 2 1

Special Thanks
Chris Goddard and staff at the Australian War Memorial Museum, staff at South Shields Public Library, West Australian Army Museum, and Gary Hayes for expertise on military uniforms.

*This project has been supported by ArtsWA in association with Lotterywest, and assisted by the Australian Government through the Australia Council, its arts funding and advisory body.*

Australian Government
Australia Council for the Arts
artswa
Government of Western Australia



Sources:

Adam-Smith, P, The ANZACs: The Classic Account of the Men who Gave Birth to the Legend, Penguin, Victoria, 1991.
Bean, CEW, The Story of Anzac, Angus and Robertson, Sydney, 1921.
Benson, CI, The Man with the Donkey: John Simpson Kirkpatrick, The Good Samaritan of Gallipoli, Hodder and Stoughton, London, 1965.
Buley, EC, Glorious Deeds of Australasians in the Great War, Andrew Melrose, London, 1915.
Cochrane, P, Simpson and the Donkey: the Making of a Legend, Melbourne University Press, Victoria, 1992.
Curran, T, Across The Bar, Ogmios Publications, Queensland, 1994.
Curran, T, Not Only A Hero: an Illustrated Life of Simpson, the Man with the Donkey, ANZAC Day Commemorative Committee (Queensland), 1998.
Hamilton, J, Goodbye Cobber, God Bless You, Pan Macmillan, Sydney, 2004.
King, J, Gallipoli Diaries: The Anzac's Own Story Day by Day, Kangaroo Press, NSW, 2003.
Moorehead, A, Gallipoli, Macmillan, South Melbourne, 1989.
Robertson, J, ANZAC and Empire: The Tragedy and Glory of Gallipoli, Hamlyn, Victoria, 1990.